W9-CFQ-986

FUN
with
CLAY

FUN
with
CLAY

CHERYL OWEN

JENNA BOOKS

Published by East Coast Marketing
Jenna Books
1350 Blue Hills Avenue,
Bloomfield, CT 06002.

© Salamander Books Ltd, 1994
129-137 York Way,
London N7 9LG,
United Kingdom.

ISBN 1-85600-030-3

All rights reserved. Except for use in a review,
no part of this book may be reproduced, stored in a
retrieval system or transmitted in any form or by any
means, electronic, mechanical, photocopying, recording,
or otherwise, without prior permission of the publisher.

This book may not be sold outside the
United States of America or Canada

CREDITS

Editor: Jilly Glassborow

Designer: Patrick Knowles

Photographers: Mark Gatehouse and Jonathan Pollock

Craft adviser: Leslie Thompson

Typeset by: SX Composing Ltd., Rayleigh, Essex

Color separation by: Scantrans Pte. Ltd., Singapore

Printed in Belgium by: Proost International Book Production

The author and publishers would like to thank
Peter Pan Playthings, Kembrey Park, Swindon,
for supplying the colored clay.

CONTENTS

INTRODUCTION	6
CLAY CREATURES	8
TRAIN GANG	10
HAPPY CLOWN	12
FUN MIRRORS	14
PENCIL PETS	16
DINOSAUR FRIDGE MAGNETS	18
FISH BUTTONS	20
FRUITY BROOCHES	22
JAZZY JEWELRY	24
CHRISTMAS DECORATIONS	26
NICE MICE	28
SUN AND MOON	30
PATTERNS	32

INTRODUCTION

Playing with clay and dough is always great fun, and there are plenty of different kinds to choose from. Some types of clay need to be baked in the oven to harden them – they come in a wide range of bright colors. Others harden by leaving them in the air. These clays are usually colorless and can be painted with poster paints. You can even make your own clay out of flour and salt.

Oven-Baked Clay This clay can be quite hard so you'll have to knead it with your hands to soften it up first. Then you can either model it into different shapes, or roll it out flat and cut shapes out of it with a blunt knife or modeling tool.

Models made from air-drying clay are great fun to paint

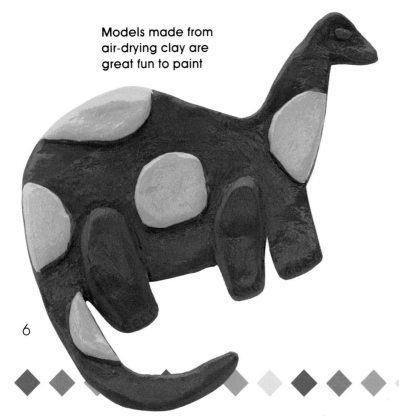

Baking Your Models If you need to bake your designs in the oven, make sure you ask an adult to help you. And always wear ovenmitts so you don't burn yourself.

6

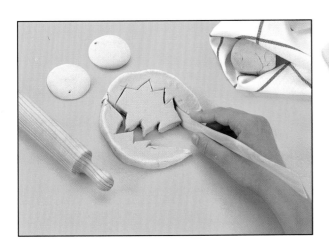

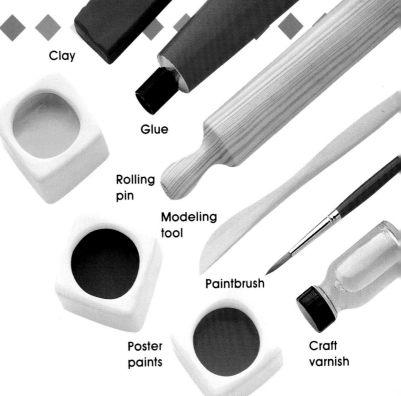

Clay

Glue

Rolling pin

Modeling tool

Paintbrush

Poster paints

Craft varnish

Air-Drying Clay Always store this clay in an airtight container to stop it going hard. And, while you are modeling, keep spare clay under a damp cloth.

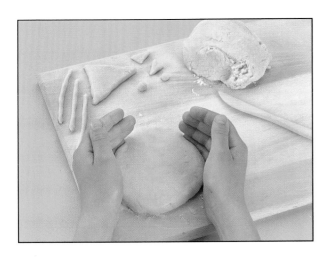

Salt Dough is easy to make – mix two cups of flour with one cup of salt and one cup of water. Knead the dough until it's smooth. With an adult's help, bake your model very slowly for about eight hours. Always give it five coats of varnish to stop it from going moldy.

Varnishing To protect your models and make them shiny, give them two coats of craft varnish (salt dough needs five). Let each coat dry before applying the next one.

7

CLAY CREATURES

These appealing creatures stand only about 2½in tall. They are made from the type of modeling clay that hardens in the oven, although you could make them out of any kind of clay. The body and head are made in the same way for each character. Follow the pictures carefully to make all the other pieces.

YOU WILL NEED

Colored clay that hardens in the oven

Craft varnish

Thick needle

Paintbrush

Rolling pin and blunt knife or modeling tool

Cookie sheet and ovenmitts

1 For each creature, roll a ball of clay 1½in wide for the body and a smaller one for the head. Mold the body into an oval and flatten the bottom so it will stand up. Press the head on top.

2 Roll a sausage of clay for the teddy's and rabbits' arms. Cut it in half and press the arms to each side of the body. Roll a ball of clay for the teddy's and

rabbit's muzzle, and small black balls for the eyes and nose. Press the pieces to the head. Mark the mouth with a needle.

3 For the teddy's ears, roll a ball of clay and cut it in half. Press the ears to the head. Then roll some blue clay out flat and cut out a scarf and knot. Wrap the scarf around the teddy's neck, overlapping the ends. Press the knot to the overlap. Roll a small ball of clay and press it on top. Press tiny balls of yellow clay onto the scarf.

4 For the rabbit's ears, roll a sausage of clay. Flatten it slightly, then cut it in half. Press the cut ends to the head and bend the ears forward. Roll some green clay out flat and cut two triangles for a bow. Press the bow onto the rabbit, adding a small ball of clay for the knot.

5 For the penguin, cut a red scarf and hat band, two black wings, and a yellow beak and feet out of rolled out clay. Mold a cone of green clay for the hat and press it onto the head. Press the other shapes in place. Finish off with two black eyes and a red pom pom for the hat.

6 Ask an adult to help you to bake the models in an oven following the instructions on the clay package. Finally, varnish your models.

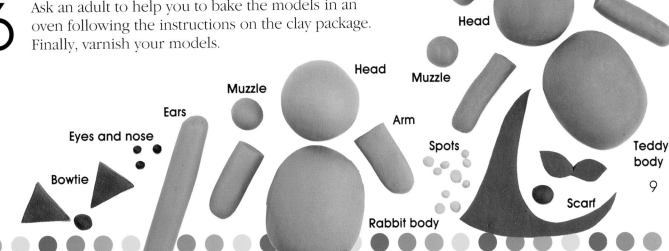

Hat

Hat band

Eyes

Pom pom

Beak

Scarf

Head

Wing

Penguin body

Scarf tails

Feet

Eyes and nose

Ear

Ear

Arm

Head

Muzzle

Head

Muzzle

Arm

Ears

Spots

Eyes and nose

Bowtie

Rabbit body

Scarf

Teddy body

9

TRAIN GANG

This colorful train set would make a delightful table centerpiece at a birthday party. It's made from modeling clay that hardens in the air. The picture below shows the actual size of the train so use it as a guide for making your own model. Or, for the exact measurements, turn to the diagram on page 32.

YOU WILL NEED

Clay that hardens in the air
Poster paints and paintbrush
Birthday cake candles
Narrow ribbon
Rolling pin
Blunt knife or modeling tool
All-purpose glue
Craft varnish

1 To make the engine, roll some clay out flat with a rolling pin until it is about 1¼in thick. Cut a rectangle for the cabin, making it about 1½in wide.

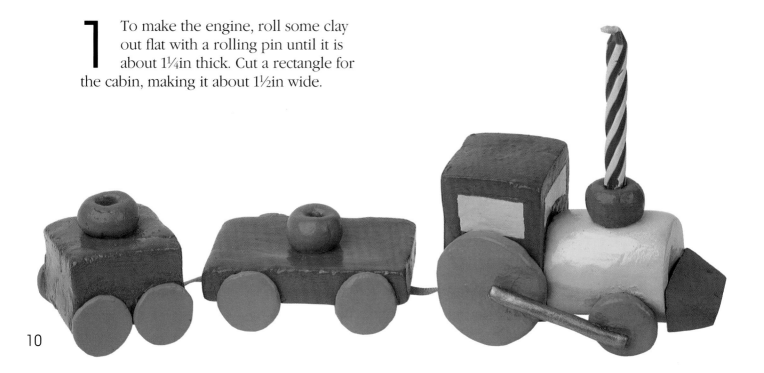

2 Roll some clay into a sausage shape, making it nearly as wide as the cabin. Cut it down to the right length for the front of the engine. Dampen one end and stick it onto the cabin.

3 Make a cow catcher by cutting a long narrow rectangle of clay to fit the width of the cabin. Carefully cut it in half diagonally. Now cut two rail cars, one long and low, the other shaped more like a cube. Make them both as wide as the cabin.

4 To make the candle holders, roll three small balls of clay. Press the end of a candle into each ball to make a hole, then remove the candle. Dampen the holders and press one onto the center of the engine for a funnel. Put the other holders on the rail cars.

5 Roll two balls of clay about ⅝in wide for the big wheels and 10 smaller balls for the small wheels. Flatten all the balls. For the axles, roll a thin sausage of clay and cut off two pieces about 1½in long.

Ribbon

6 Set the pieces aside for a few days to harden, then paint them. When the paint is dry, add a couple of coats of varnish. Next, glue the wheels and axles into place and stick the cow catcher to the front of the engine.

7 Join the rail cars to the cabin by gluing a length of ribbon underneath. Finally, place a candle in the funnel. Place candles in the other holders if you are using your train as a centerpiece for a birthday party. Remember never to leave a burning candle unattended.

Poster
paints
and
brush

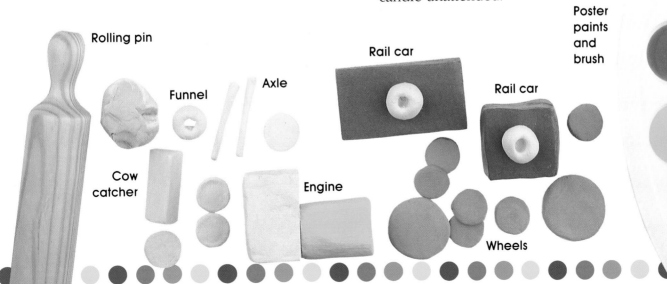

Rolling pin

Funnel

Axle

Rail car

Rail car

Cow
catcher

Engine

Wheels

HAPPY CLOWN

This cheerful fellow makes a useful paperweight to help keep your stationery in place. He is made from salt dough, brightly colored with poster paints.

YOU WILL NEED

2 cups of all-purpose flour

1 cup of salt

1 cup of water

Poster paints

Paintbrush

Craft varnish

Pastry board and rolling pin

Blunt knife or modeling tool

Bowl and wooden spoon

Cookie sheet and ovenmitts

1 To make the salt dough, put the flour and salt in a bowl and gradually stir in the water. Mix all the ingredients together with a wooden spoon, then knead it until you have a soft dough.

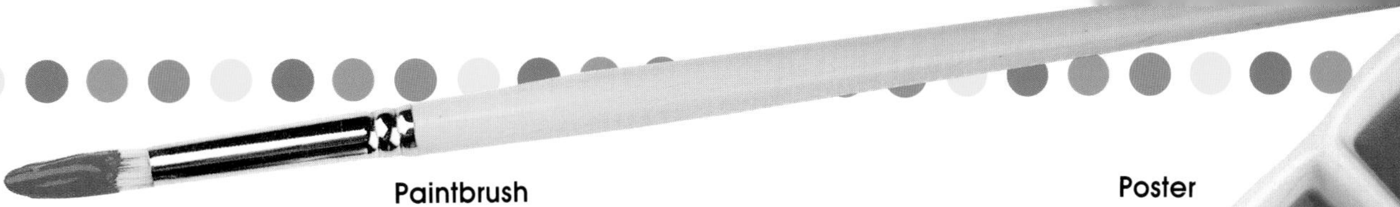

Paintbrush

Poster paints

2 Place your dough on a lightly floured pastry board. Roll a ball of dough about 2½in wide for the head. Roll another ball about 1in wide for the nose. Flatten the head, then gently press the nose onto the center.

3 Roll the remaining dough out flat. Using a blunt knife, and following the picture below, cut a hat, a heart, two eyes, and a mouth out of dough. Press all the pieces to the head.

4 Now roll two small balls for the cheeks and two for the eyeballs. Press these onto the head too.

5 Finally, roll several thin sausages of dough for the hair. Cut the hair into short pieces and press it onto each side of the head.

6 Carefully place your clown on a cookie sheet and ask an adult to help you bake it in the oven at 250°F. Bake it slowly for about eight hours or until it is really hard. Remove the clown from the oven and leave it to cool.

7 Mix your poster paints into different colors and paint the clown brightly. Finally, when the paint is dry, varnish the clown all over five times, allowing the varnish to dry between coats.

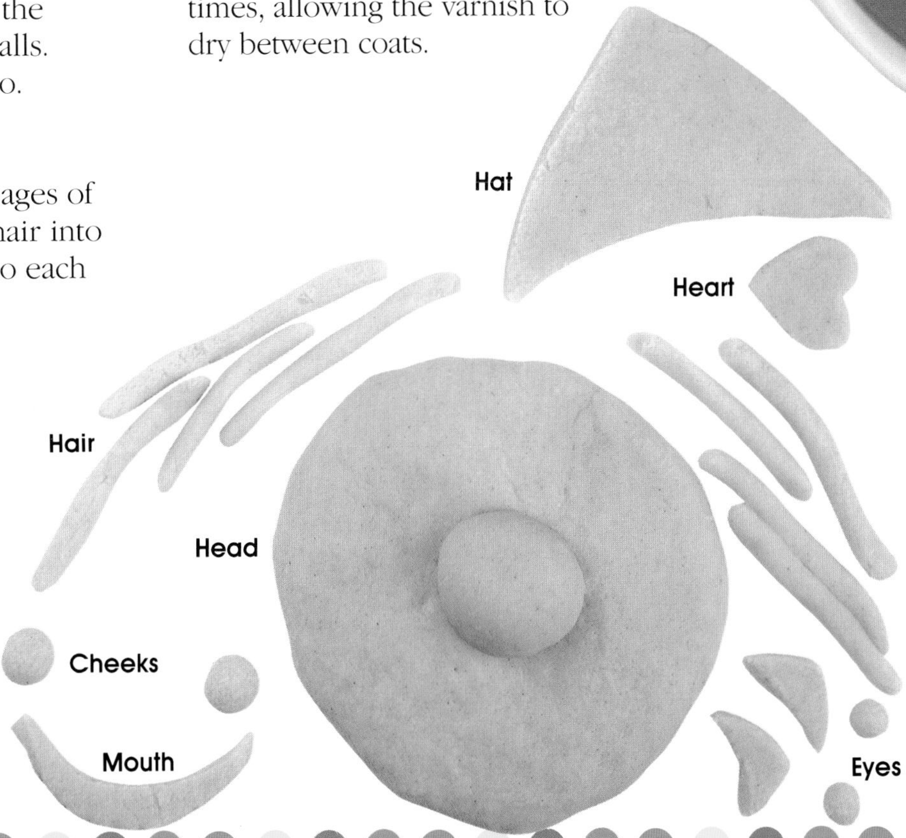

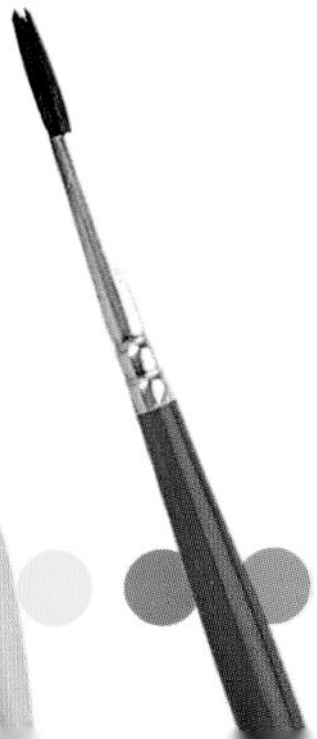

Hat

Heart

Hair

Head

Craft varnish

Paintbrush

Cheeks

Mouth

Eyes

Fun Mirrors

These nifty mirrors will brighten up any room, and would make great gifts for family and friends. You can make your mirror frames as large or small as you like – these measure 7in × 5½in.

YOU WILL NEED

Clay that hardens in the oven
Rolling pin
Modeling tool or blunt knife
Ruler
Pencil
Pocket mirror
Craft varnish
All-purpose glue
Picture hanger
Cookie sheet and ovenmitts

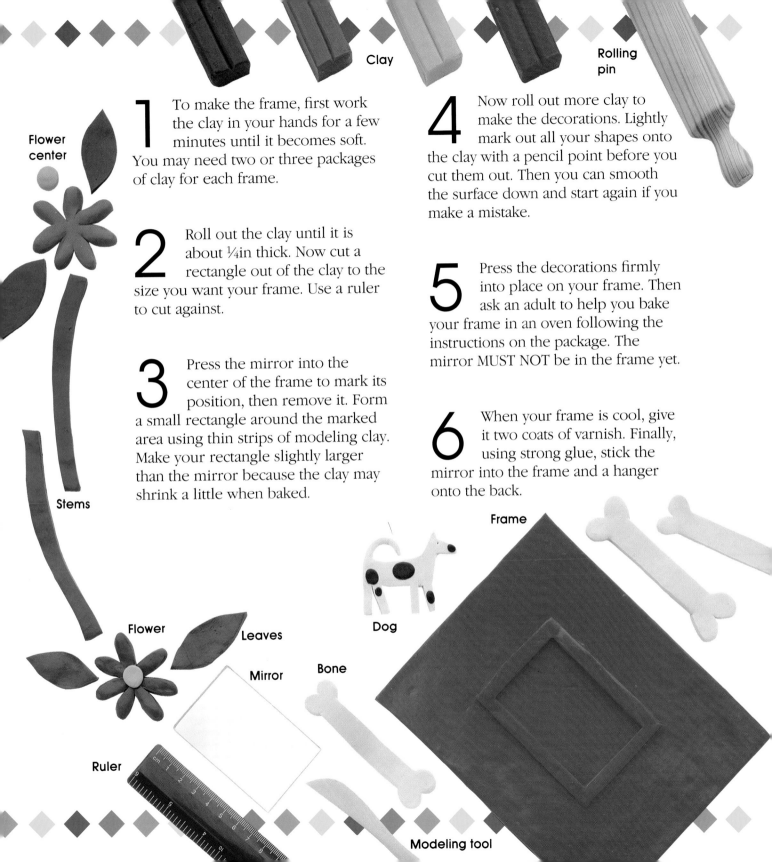

Clay

Rolling pin

Flower center

1 To make the frame, first work the clay in your hands for a few minutes until it becomes soft. You may need two or three packages of clay for each frame.

2 Roll out the clay until it is about ¼in thick. Now cut a rectangle out of the clay to the size you want your frame. Use a ruler to cut against.

3 Press the mirror into the center of the frame to mark its position, then remove it. Form a small rectangle around the marked area using thin strips of modeling clay. Make your rectangle slightly larger than the mirror because the clay may shrink a little when baked.

4 Now roll out more clay to make the decorations. Lightly mark out all your shapes onto the clay with a pencil point before you cut them out. Then you can smooth the surface down and start again if you make a mistake.

5 Press the decorations firmly into place on your frame. Then ask an adult to help you bake your frame in an oven following the instructions on the package. The mirror MUST NOT be in the frame yet.

6 When your frame is cool, give it two coats of varnish. Finally, using strong glue, stick the mirror into the frame and a hanger onto the back.

Stems

Flower

Leaves

Mirror

Bone

Dog

Frame

Ruler

Modeling tool

PENCIL PETS

These amazing creatures look great sitting on top of your pencils. Made from colored clay that hardens in the oven, the models have been given a coat of glossy varnish to make them shine. Once you've made these, see if you can make up some of your own designs.

1 Start by rolling a ball of clay 1in wide for each creature. Mold the ball for the turtle into an oval. Squeeze one side of the ball for the porcupine to a point to make a snout.

YOU WILL NEED

Colored clay that hardens
   in the oven
Thick needle
Pencil
Rolling pin
Craft varnish and paintbrush
Blunt knife or modeling tool
Cookie sheet and ovenmitts

Craft varnish

2 Make a hole for the pencil in each creature. Push the pencil point into the body to start the hole, then push in the top of the pencil.

3 For the turtle, mold four small ovals of clay for the legs and a small triangle for the tail. Roll another, larger ball for the head; pull one side out to make a neck. Now press all the pieces in place under the body. Mark the shell pattern with a needle.

4 For the frog, roll some green clay out flat with a rolling pin and cut out some webbed feet following the shape shown below. Stamp a hole in the middle of the feet with the top of a pencil and press the frog's body on top, matching the holes.

5 Roll two small balls of green clay and press them on top of the frog for the eye sockets. Make tiny eyes from black and white clay and press them into place. Draw a smiling mouth with a needle.

6 For the porcupine, roll tiny balls of black clay for the eyes and nose. Press them into place. Then mark quills all over the body with a needle.

7 To make the owl's wings, mold a ball of clay into an oval and cut it in half. Squeeze each half into a point at one end. Roll two small ovals of clay for the claws and a diamond shape for the beak. Press all the pieces onto the owl. Make tiny eyes from black and white clay.

8 Ask an adult to help you to bake the models in an oven following the directions on the package. Finally, varnish your models.

Rolling pin

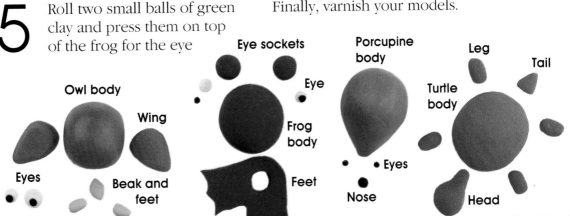

Owl body • Wing • Eyes • Beak and feet • Eye sockets • Eye • Frog body • Feet • Porcupine body • Eyes • Nose • Leg • Tail • Turtle body • Head

17

DINOSAUR FRIDGE MAGNETS

These bright dinosaurs will lumber colorfully across your fridge door. The three shown here are Brontosaurus, Tyrannosaurus Rex, and Stegosaurus. Do you know which one is which?

YOU WILL NEED

Clay that hardens in the air

Rolling pin

Blunt knife or modeling tool

Pencil

Poster paints

Paintbrush

Varnish

Small fridge magnets

All-purpose glue

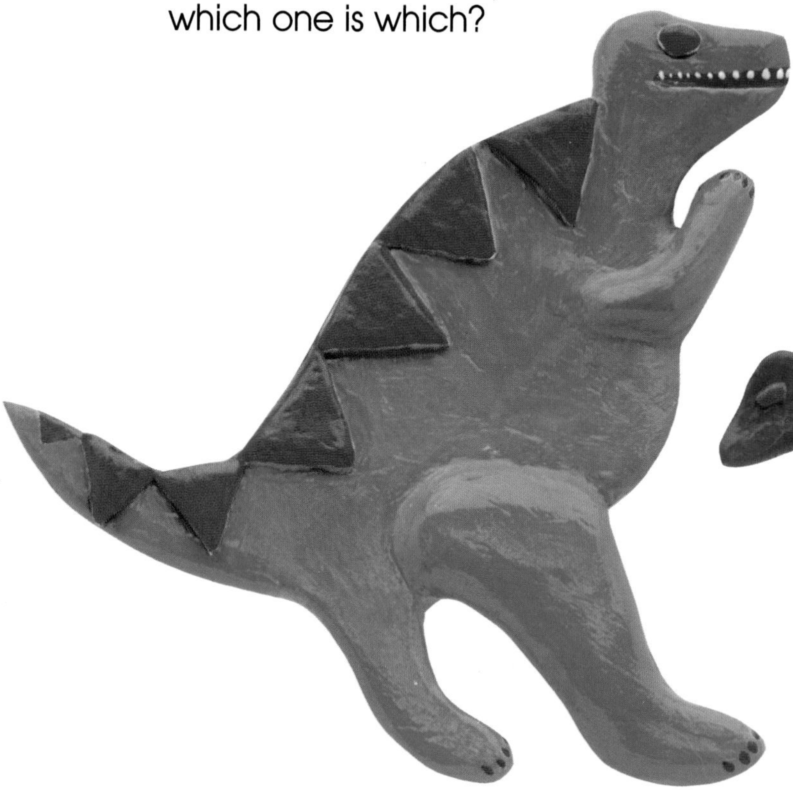

1 Break off a large piece of clay and knead it with your hands until it is smooth. Form the clay into a ball, then roll it out until it is about ¼in thick.

2 Lightly mark a dinosaur shape onto the clay with a pencil point. You can experiment first with different dinosaur shapes on a piece of paper if you like. Now cut the shape out with a blunt knife or modeling tool.

3 Model the dinosaurs' eyes, spots and spines from small pieces of clay. Press them into position. Now mold extra clay onto the legs to give a 3-D effect. Leave your dinosaur to dry.

4 When the clay has dried thoroughly, paint your dinosaur with brightly colored poster paints. Allow one color to dry before painting the next one.

5 When the paint is dry, seal your model with two coats of varnish. Finally, stick a small fridge magnet onto the back of your dinosaur with strong glue.

6 Once you've made these dinosaurs you could create some designs of your own. How about making a Spinosaurus or a Triceratops? A good book on dinosaurs will give you plenty of ideas.

Paintbrush

Poster paints

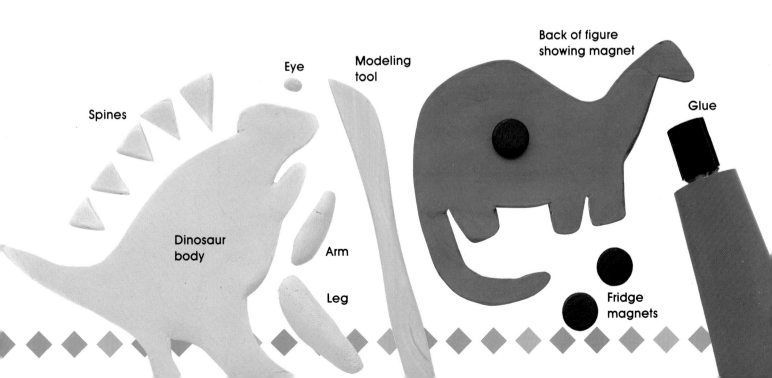

Spines

Eye

Modeling tool

Dinosaur body

Arm

Leg

Back of figure showing magnet

Glue

Fridge magnets

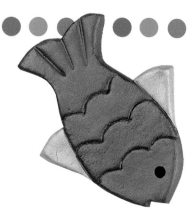

Fish Buttons

This school of fancy fish buttons and matching badge would look great on a cardigan or jacket. Sew the buttons to clothing that does not need to be unbuttoned often – the fish are not suitable for a lot of wear and tear and cannot be washed. They are made from modeling clay that hardens in the air, and have been painted with shiny pearlized paints.

YOU WILL NEED

Clay that hardens in the air

Pearlized craft paints

Black poster paint

Paintbrushes

Thick needle

Brooch pin

All-purpose glue

Tracing paper, pencil, and scissors

Rolling pin

  Blunt knife or modeling tool

1 Knead some clay with your hands until it is soft. Remember to keep clay you are not using in an airtight container or under a damp cloth so that it doesn't get hard.

2 Roll the clay out flat using a rolling pin. Then cut lots of fish shapes using a blunt knife. You can either do this freehand, marking the shape first with a pencil point, or you can trace the patterns from page 32. Cut the patterns out, lay them onto the clay and cut around them.

3 Using a thick needle, make two holes in the middle of the buttons about ⅛in apart. You can also add details such as fish scales. Leave the fish to dry.

4 Paint the buttons and brooch with pearlized paints. Then use a fine brush to paint the eyes and mouth using black paint. When the paint is dry, glue the brooch pin to the back of the badge.

Black poster paint

Paintbrush

Pearlized paints

Glue

Unpainted buttons

Brooch pin

Back of brooch showing pin

Cutting out a button

21

FRUITY BROOCHES

Jazz up a sweater or jacket with these fun fruity brooches. They are made out of the type of modeling clay that you have to bake in the oven to harden. Make sure you get an adult to help you to use the oven, and be very careful not to burn yourself. The clay can be very hard to work at first. Keep molding it in your hands until it begins to soften.

YOU WILL NEED

Colored clay that hardens
   in the oven
Varnish and paintbrush
Brooch pin and glue
Rolling pin
Cookie sheet and ovenmitts

1 To make a banana, roll a piece of yellow clay into a sausage shape and round off the ends. Bend the clay into a banana shape and add a small piece of black clay to one end for the stalk.

2 For the strawberry, roll a ball of red clay about 1½in wide. Cut the ball in half and mold one of the halves into a strawberry shape.

22

3 Roll some green clay out flat. Following the shape below, cut out a leaf shape and press this firmly on top of the strawberry.

4 Roll a thin green sausage for the stalk and press this in place on top of the leaf. Finally, make little cuts in the surface of the strawberry using a pin.

5 For the apple, roll a green ball about 1½in wide and cut it in half. Put a small dent in the top of one of the halves to make an apple shape. Then make leaves and a stalk as you did for the strawberry. Press all the pieces together.

6 Roll about 25-30 small blue balls for the grapes. Roll a larger ball about 1in wide and cut it in half. Press the grapes onto the front of one of the halves to form a bunch. Make green leaves and a brown stem as before and press them into place.

7 Ask an adult to help you to bake the fruits in the oven, carefully following the instructions on the package. When the fruits have cooled, give them a coat of varnish to make them shine. Finally, glue a brooch pin to the back of each brooch.

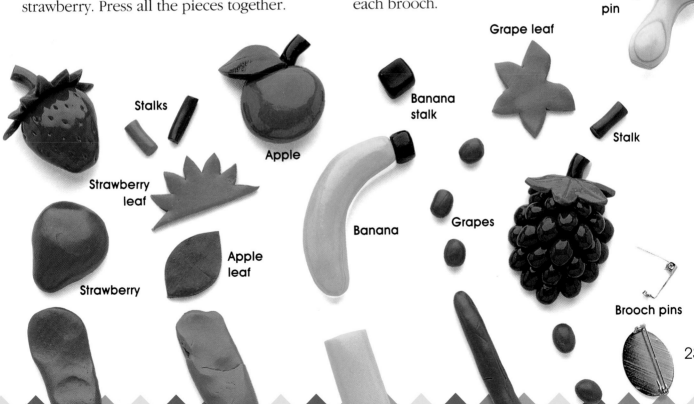

Craft varnish

Paintbrush

Rolling pin

Stalks

Strawberry leaf

Strawberry

Apple leaf

Apple

Banana

Banana stalk

Grapes

Grape leaf

Stalk

Brooch pins

23

JAZZY JEWELRY

This jazzy jewelry set will look good with any outfit. It's made from air-drying clay, but you could use salt dough instead (see the recipe on page 7).

YOU WILL NEED

Clay that hardens in the air

Blunt knife or modeling tool

Knitting needle

Rolling pin

Pencil

Poster paints and paintbrush

Craft varnish

Length of cord

Brooch pin

   All-purpose glue

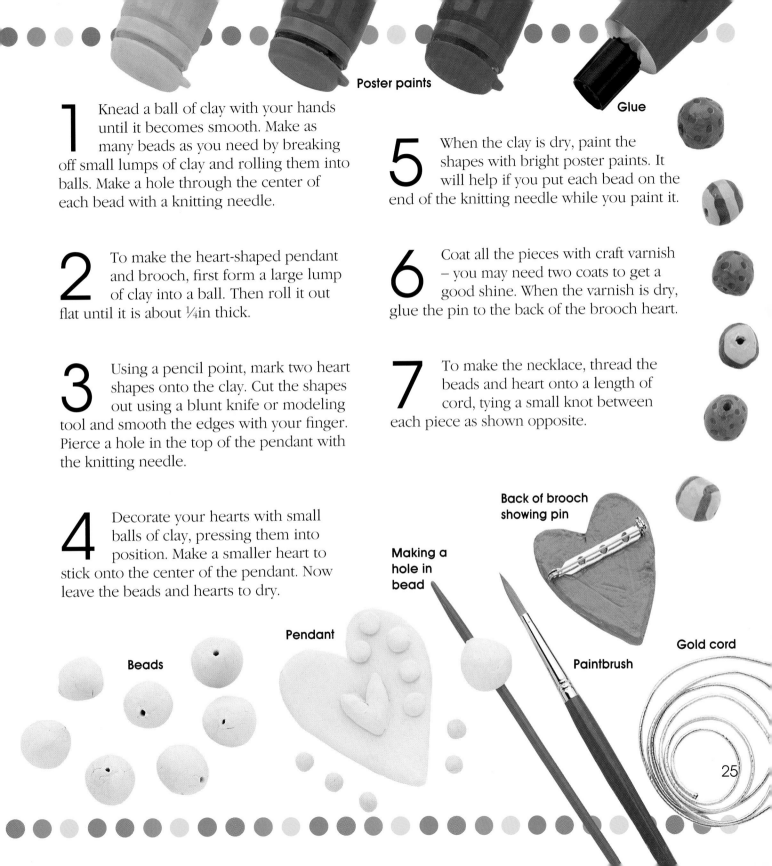

Glue

1 Knead a ball of clay with your hands until it becomes smooth. Make as many beads as you need by breaking off small lumps of clay and rolling them into balls. Make a hole through the center of each bead with a knitting needle.

2 To make the heart-shaped pendant and brooch, first form a large lump of clay into a ball. Then roll it out flat until it is about ¼in thick.

3 Using a pencil point, mark two heart shapes onto the clay. Cut the shapes out using a blunt knife or modeling tool and smooth the edges with your finger. Pierce a hole in the top of the pendant with the knitting needle.

4 Decorate your hearts with small balls of clay, pressing them into position. Make a smaller heart to stick onto the center of the pendant. Now leave the beads and hearts to dry.

5 When the clay is dry, paint the shapes with bright poster paints. It will help if you put each bead on the end of the knitting needle while you paint it.

6 Coat all the pieces with craft varnish – you may need two coats to get a good shine. When the varnish is dry, glue the pin to the back of the brooch heart.

7 To make the necklace, thread the beads and heart onto a length of cord, tying a small knot between each piece as shown opposite.

Back of brooch showing pin

Making a hole in bead

Pendant

Beads

Gold cord

Paintbrush

25

CHRISTMAS DECORATIONS

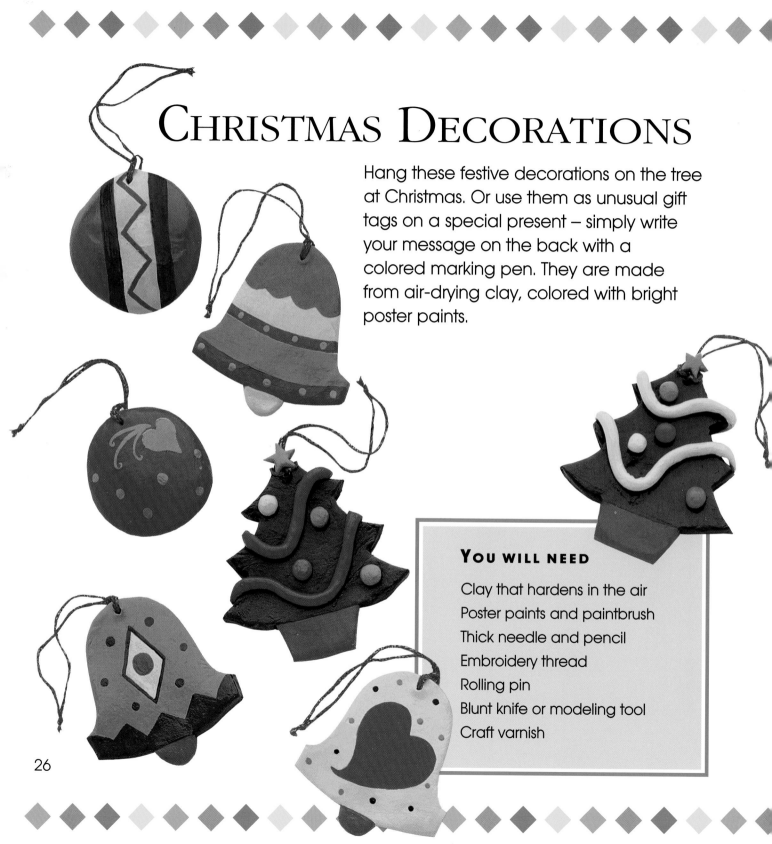

Hang these festive decorations on the tree at Christmas. Or use them as unusual gift tags on a special present – simply write your message on the back with a colored marking pen. They are made from air-drying clay, colored with bright poster paints.

YOU WILL NEED

Clay that hardens in the air
Poster paints and paintbrush
Thick needle and pencil
Embroidery thread
Rolling pin
Blunt knife or modeling tool
Craft varnish

1 Knead some clay with your hands until it is smooth. To make a tree ball, roll a piece of clay into a ball about 1½in wide, then flatten it. Pierce a small hole close to the edge with a thick needle.

2 To make a Christmas tree, roll some clay out flat with a rolling pin. Mark out a tree shape and a small star using a pencil point and cut the shapes out with a blunt knife or modeling tool.

3 Press the star on top of the tree. Then roll long sausages of clay for the garlands and small balls for the tiny tree balls. Dampen the tree slightly and press the garlands and balls into place. Pierce a small hole just below the star.

Rolling pin

Paintbrush

4 For the bell, roll some clay out flat and mark out a bell shape. Cut it out and pierce a hole at the top.

5 Make up lots more decorations in the same way. Then set them all aside to harden. When the clay is dry, paint the shapes with bright poster paints.

Poster paint

6 When the paint is dry, give your decorations two coats of varnish. Finally, hang them on lengths of embroidery thread.

Cutting out the Christmas tree

Modeling tool

Garland for tree

Ball decorations for tree

Star for tree

Embroidery thread

27

NICE MICE

This trio of rosy-colored mice would make a lovely gift, either as a set or individually. The mice are made from salt dough using basic kitchen ingredients, and the eyes and nose are made of whole cloves. You'll need to bake the mice in the oven for about eight hours to make them set hard. Ask an adult to help you to do this.

Supper!

YOU WILL NEED

2 cups of all-purpose flour

I cup of salt

1 cup of water

3 whole cloves for each mouse

Poster paints and paintbrush

Craft varnish

All-purpose glue

Narrow ribbon and scissors

Bowl and wooden spoon

Pastry board

Cookie sheet and ovenmitts

1 To make the salt dough, put the flour and salt in a bowl and gradually stir in the water. Mix all the ingredients together using a wooden spoon, then knead it until you have a soft dough. Place the dough on a lightly floured pastry board.

2 To make a large mouse, roll a ball of dough about 2in wide. Roll smaller balls of dough for the medium-sized and the small mouse. Squeeze one side of each ball into a point to make the nose.

3 For each mouse, mold two small balls of dough for the ears. Flatten the balls into ear shapes and press them gently onto the heads.

4 Push a clove into the shaped end for a nose, then push cloves into each side of the head for the eyes.

5 Place your mice on a cookie sheet and ask an adult to help you to bake them in an oven at 250°F. Bake them for about eight hours or until they are really hard. Remove the mice from the oven and set them aside to cool.

6 Mix the poster paints into different shades of pink and paint your mice brightly. Or you can color your mice in more natural shades of brown and beige.

7 When the paint is dry, varnish the mice completely five times, allowing the varnish to dry between coats. Finally, glue a length of ribbon onto the base of each mouse for the tail.

Glue

Scissors

Ribbon for tails

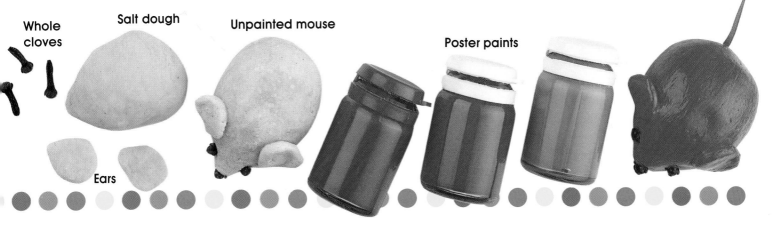

Whole cloves

Salt dough

Unpainted mouse

Poster paints

Ears

SUN AND MOON

Hang this happy smiling sun on the wall to brighten up a dull room. Or make a glittering crescent moon to decorate a trinket or gift box. Both pieces are made from modeling clay that hardens in the air. Bright jewelry stones have been glued onto them to make them really shine.

YOU WILL NEED

Clay that hardens in the air
Poster paints and paintbrush
Craft varnish
Jewelry stones
Thick needle
All-purpose glue
Tracing paper, pencil, and scissors
Rolling pin and blunt knife

Poster paints

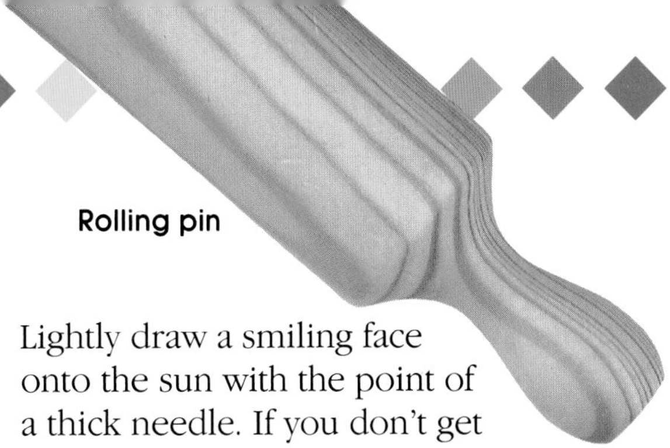

Rolling pin

1 Roll the clay out flat until it is about ¼in thick. Then lightly mark out a moon shape using the point of a pencil or thick needle. Cut out the moon with a blunt knife.

4 Lightly draw a smiling face onto the sun with the point of a thick needle. If you don't get your drawing right the first time, you can gently stroke away the lines with a finger. When you are happy, redraw over the face with the needle, making the lines deeper.

2 To make the sun, you can either draw the shape freehand or trace it from page 32. Cut your pattern out and lay it onto the clay to cut around.

5 Leave the models to harden, then paint them in bright poster paints. When the paint is dry, varnish your models. Finally, glue small jewelry stones onto the moon and the sun rays.

Ball of clay for face

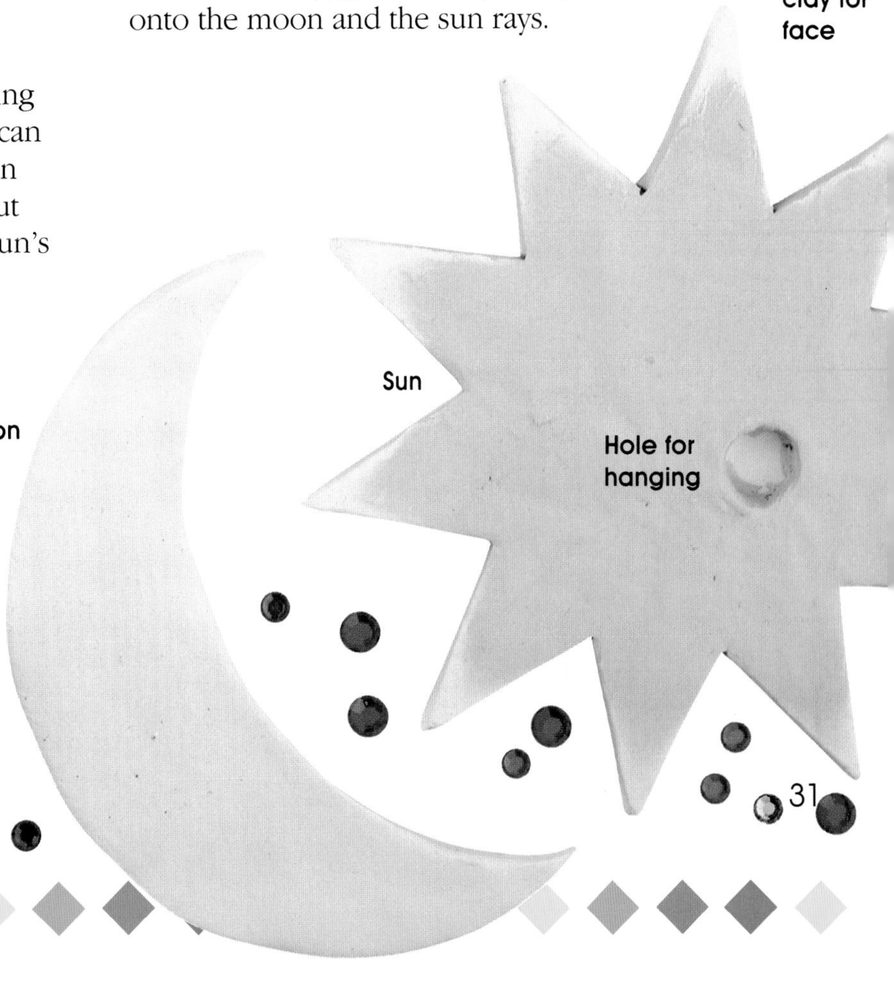

3 Cut a small hole in the sun, making it off center as shown here. You can use this hole later to hang the sun on your wall. Now roll a ball of clay about 1¼in wide. Flatten the ball to make the sun's face. Dampen the back of the face, then press it onto the middle of the sun.

Sun

Moon

Hole for hanging

Glue

Jewels

31

PATTERNS

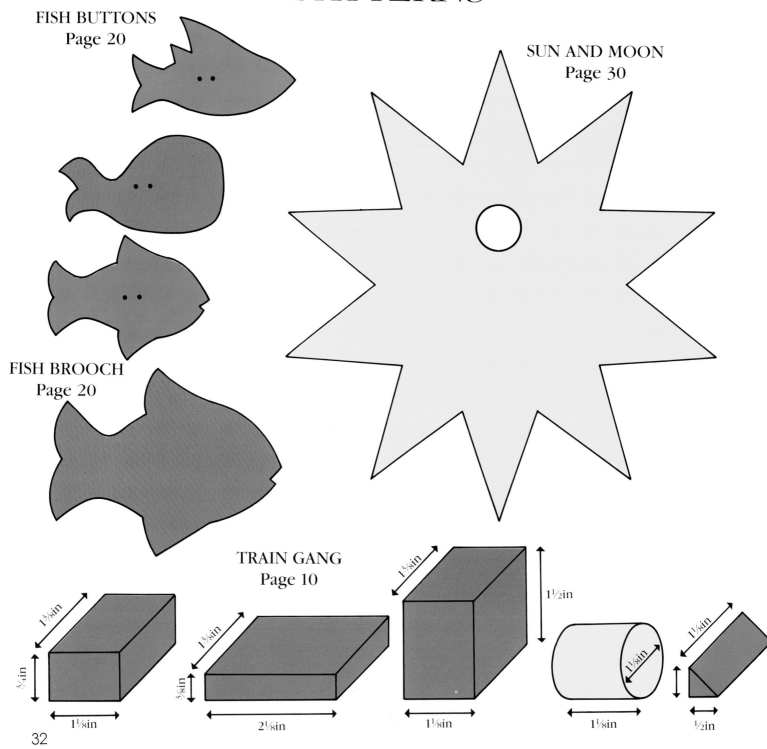

FISH BUTTONS
Page 20

FISH BROOCH
Page 20

SUN AND MOON
Page 30

TRAIN GANG
Page 10

1³/₈in

³/₄in

1¹/₈in

1³/₈in

³/₈in

2¹/₈in

1³/₈in

1¹/₂in

1¹/₈in

1¹/₈in

1¹/₈in

1¹/₈in

¹/₂in

32